Day and Night

Story by Rebel Williams
Illustrations by Kris Wiltse

In the day you can
see the sun,

and at night you can
see the moon.

3

In the day you can see clouds,

4

and at night you can
see stars.

In the day you can see a plane,

and at night you can
see a comet.

In the day you can
see an eagle,

and at night you can
see an owl.

In the day you can see birds,

and at night you can see bats.

In the day you can
see a mountain lion,

and at night you can
see a jaguar.

Sometimes the day

becomes like the night.

That's a total eclipse!